Saltford Memories

Night Raids, Nightingales a

Friends of Saltford Library

First published in Great Britain in 2015 by Friends of Saltford Library and Bath and North East Somerset Council Libraries.

This 2nd edition published 2015 by Bath and North East Somerset Libraries Press

A CIP catalogue record for this book is held by the British Library.

Printed by Whitehall Printing, Barton Hill, Bristol

Acknowledgements

We would like to thank everyone who offered their memories whether in writing or within the many vibrant discussions which have taken place during the time of material gathering for this book.

We would especially like to pay tribute to Sue Brock who sadly passed away before this book came to full fruition. Sue was an important part of the fabric of Saltford and a stalwart of the memories sessions and the Friends of Saltford Library.

We are hugely grateful to the local artists who produced the original illustrations specifically for this publication:

Sue Macey of Avon Valley Artists (Saltford Church Hall)

James King

Jo Mckenna

We should also like to offer our huge appreciation to Bath and N.E. Somerset Arts Development team for the grant they awarded for this project, without which this publication could never have happened, to Bath and N.E. Somerset Library Service for their input and to Saltford Community Association for all their practical support and encouragement.

Introduction

There have previously been a number of publications about the history of Saltford village. This book doesn't have any aspirations of being a factual record of dates and happenings but is a view of past times in Saltford through the memories of local people. It is a fascinating re-construction. We are aware that memory is a complex process and facts are often elusive. We hope that this publication is part of a wider process and will help other lost memories to re-surface. Different people's memories of the same event can sometimes be contradictory but this is what makes the whole process exciting and alive. This publication is about people's personal experiences of Saltford and so gives a valuable insight into what it *felt* like to be there then – moments frozen in time.

Having become immersed in other people's memories of this village, the Saltford of the past has become very vivid for both Cynthia and myself. If I shut my eyes now in Saltford Library, where I am typing these words, I can feel that I am in Mattick's store (as the library once was) – the smell of paraffin and the bell above the door ready to clang. If I shut my eyes I can imagine, amongst the flow of traffic that I might catch a glimpse of Sister Touhig (a cigarette hanging from her mouth) as she drives to the next home confinement.

Cynthia and I both admitted to each other while bringing this book together, that we felt an envy for those Saltford people who had lived all their lives here, many of whom have had connections with this unique place for a number of generations.

Bath and N.E. Somerset Library Service are proud to have been involved in re-capturing these fascinating anecdotes and personal memoirs of an ever evolving village.

Cynthia Wilson (Chair of the Friends of Saltford Library)

and June Wentland (Reader Development Officer, Bath and N.E. Somerset Library Service)

Contents

Chapter One - Village Life
Floods, freezes and subterfuge at the village carnival

Chapter Two - Village Characters
A car with stained glass windows, the amazing Saltford 'water-cycle' and the nicotine-fingered mid-wife with dubious beauty tips

Chapter Three - Railways and Transport
Hot cinders, 'Hetty the railway hen' and five shilling motor bikes

Chapter Four - The River, Farms and Wildlife
Eel traps, ice –skating and rowing regattas

Chapter Five - The Second World War
Stock-piling shopkeepers, pitch-forks and secret missions

Chapter Six - Childhood, School, Scouts and Guides
Dame schools, gas lamps and Waltzing Matilda

Chapter Seven - Village Buildings
Sing songs at the Manor House, ancient light bulbs, and a lady named 'Fluff'

Chapter Eight - Recent Years
Buzzards, road closures and proposals of marriage

Chapter One - Village Life

Floods, freezes and subterfuge at the village carnival

At one time many villages were self-contained, self-reliant entities in a way in which they no longer are. Saltford was no exception with its own full range of shops some of which were stocked with goods from the local farms, and a social calendar which included such events as the annual carnival.

In the 1930s Trevor Ewins remembers the rural atmosphere of the village: "There were three working farms and there were many established amenities. The church and the chapel, the golf course, three pubs, cricket and football teams, rowing clubs and Women's Institute, which provided many social events in the hut at the bottom of Norman Road. Saltford was at that time well served with shops – butcher, cobbler, baker, a dairy, two general stores and newsagents and hairdressers."

Ivor Stabbins moved to Saltford in 1928 when he was two years old. His mum worked hard at home doing washing for a couple of people and going out cleaning for two mornings a week besides working for Miss Wills.

"When I was at Keynsham School I remember that on Monday, when we got home, Mum would just be clearing up after a day's washing. At that time we had a boiler with a coal fire under it, so the ashes had to be cleaned out from it, in addition to all the other tidying up. Our usual tea on wash days would be a cold joint of meat with bubble and squeak, as there had been no time to prepare anything more elaborate. Still, that went down well and I can never remember being hungry.

Where we lived we often had a visit from a tramp asking if Mum could make some tea for him in his billy can. They were never refused and always went away with a nice piece of cake or a cheese sandwich. I think these tramps had a code which they left for one another outside the gate of a person who would not turn them away empty handed."

Ivor Stabbins' grandpa worked on a local farm and he remembers that his granny was: "a little lady quite well educated and as children we had great times when we visited her. She always played games with us, sometimes with cards or Blind Man's Buff. Her memory was very good and she loved poetry. The house only had paraffin oil lamps for lighting. I remember being there when Mr Skuse, the man from the hardware shop, called with his horse and cart. From this he supplied the oil and any hardware brushes, buckets and soap. The soap that was used for washing clothes was a hard 'Puritan' type supplied in a long bar. One thing that stands out in my mind was seeing this Mr Skuse cutting a piece of this soap using the jagged edge of a tin.

I just about remember Granny being ill in bed and then she died on the 17th April 1933. I was almost 7 years old at the time, and remember seeing her in her coffin in her front room."

Jeanne King moved to Saltford as a young mum in the early 1950s: "We moved into a new house in the Broadway in December 1952. Most of our neighbours had children, so we were blessed with having lots of playmates for our family of eventually three. They had the freedom to wander the fields in front of us with their friends. The highlight of the year was the Flower Show when a huge marquee was erected where the Community Centre now stands. Delightful smells of fruit and flowers greeted us. Judging was for flowers, fruit, vegetables, cakes, miniature gardens, dressmaking and knitting. The great excitement for the children was the fancy dress parade. Susan Brock's father supplied a flatbed lorry for all the children to ride around the village on – no Health and Safety in those days – nor any accidents, then back to the fields for judging."

Marie Carder also remembers the Flower Show: "Each September was the annual Flower Show, held in a large marquee erected on the fields at the back of Saltford Hall. The trestle tables were set up and flowers, vegetables, cakes miniature gardens, handwriting and all manner of jams and chutneys would be arranged in the morning for the judging. At around 2pm the Flower Show would open and locals and visitors would spend some time looking around to see who had won what. At about 5.30pm the remaining produce would be auctioned and we would carry off our 'bargains'".

Marie also has happy memories of the fancy dress parade: "We used to dress up in fancy dress and assemble by the school. We were put onto the flat bed lorries (I think loaned from Tate and Lyle) and set off in a procession around the village. We went up the High street, along Norman Road, along the main road, back down Beech road and then to the playing fields behind Saltford Hall. It probably wouldn't be allowed now but it was great fun. When we arrived the judging took place. I well remember one year running home and missing it!"

Audrey Guthrie organised the Christian Aid Carnival procession: "I usually came up with a slogan, a cryptic message which I thought funny and apt. One of the early themes was Sports – the slogan 'Play Up, Play Up and Play the Game'. Ollis lent us a flatbed lorry, we sat on bales of straw, because I worked in the farm shop at Stratham Farm, John Douglas let me have straw bales to sit on which I fetched back in my Traveller. We decorated the lorry, dressing up with anything sporty; props were tennis rackets, hockey sticks etc.

The lorry arrived in the High Street. We made friends with the driver who went off for a pint while the lorry was being decorated.

What happened to the parade of floats? A question was raised, was the lorry insured? I made enquiries. The usual Church insurance didn't cover it. Insurers were horrified that children sat on a lorry without safety harness and drove along a main road. So that was the end of the carnival procession."

Many Saltford residents have very happy memories of the Flower Show and it would appear that some people took the competitions very seriously. It has been said that if vegetable prize entries were set up in the marquee on the proceeding day then boy scouts slept there to guard it and stop any subterfuge!

There was also scandal one year when it was discovered that one lady entering the cake competition (in which everyone had to use the same recipe including the same standard number of eggs) was found to have cheated by using double -yolked eggs!

At one time the village also had an annual cricket competition. Some local residents said that they had heard that this cricket competition was held in memory of a former Prince of Wales who was killed by a cricket ball! This sounded an unlikely story but sure enough there does at least appear to have been a Prince of Wales who was struck on the head and killed by a cricket ball. This was Frederick Prince of Wales and his unfortunate accident happened in 1751. His father was George 2nd.

Frances Riley moved to Saltford in 1961: "My husband Michael, myself and Patsy, our Labrador, moved to our Victorian house with thirteen steps up to the front door overlooking the 'Bird in Hand'. Voices floated up to us from the High Street where some of the 'old families' lived. One shouted to a window cleaner, 'Anyone moved in up there?' pointing to our house. 'Yes,' he said. 'But they don't have a car.' And so we were dismissed!"

The weather has sometimes made village life very difficult. Frances recollects the 'big freeze' of 1962 /1963:

"Snow was piled high everywhere. It was sunny and extremely cold and continued until the end of March. Unfortunately the mains water supply froze underneath some roads. The water cart stopped each day outside the old school room. The folks who lived on The Batch were without water for six weeks. I carried pails of water each day to some of my neighbours. Old Barry Barton who lived in Collins Buildings came to my back door to collect water for a neighbour who lived on the corner of The Batch. Harry loved doing this as I let him smoke his pipe in the conservatory, which he wasn't allowed to do at home."

Frances also gives an account of the floods of 1968: "These were very serious floods particularly in Keynsham. Mr and Mrs Fitzer had recently moved to 'Meadowcroft' on The Shallows side of my house. Their rear garden was very steep. On the evening of the rain, spring water flooded across their large kitchen and dining room and out of the front door. It was not until the following morning that the Fire Brigade were able to pump out the water. I went to see if I could do anything to help and Mrs Fitzer gave me a trug of red roses."

Shops

Paraffin, ration books and 'lunch tongue'

Sheila Hall came to Saltford: "when it was a close knit community and so many were related to each other.

13

Garland's (general grocers) was in the High Street with a fish and chip shop next door run by Baden Brown, our local postman. This later became a sweet shop run by Mrs Stiles. By the post box was a stamp machine offering two values of stamps. We were fortunate to have milk, bread, meat, and fruit and vegetables all available to our door. The mobile library parked opposite The Bird in Hand. Coal was delivered to the sidings at Saltford Station and collected by various coal merchants."

It was from Garland's shop that Donald Reakes (mentioned in 'Saltford Characters') used to deliver people's grocery orders. Jeanne King remembers this clearly "Mr Reakes called at our house every Thursday to take an order which was delivered next day."

Pat Wood remembers the shops in Saltford in the 1940s:

"Saltford then had a baker (Batstones), a butcher and an ironmonger (now the library) and a greengrocer (now the day nursery).

On the other side of the road was the Central Store (grocer), Pope's garage which consisted of a very tiny building where Mrs Pope had an electric cooker and she used to make the most delicious gingerbread. Further on was the post office, the chemists run by B.J. Nichols, the wool shop which also housed a hairdresser, the Co-Op and a fishmonger. In the High Street was another grocer and a paper and sweet shop owned by a Mrs Stiles. Mrs Croft owned what is now Saltford News, it was then a very small shop and she held the ration books of many Saltford residents."

Marie Carder remembers the shops in the 50s and 60s:

"At the bottom of Beech Road, where the war memorial is now, there used to be some small units, one of which was a cobbler. I remember going in there, and the smell of leather.

The parade of shops on Bath Road that still exists has not changed very much, just the mix of shops. The Post Office was there, though before my time it had been at the 'Brass Knocker' on the High Street. There was a chemist and a draper's shop with a small hairdressers shop at the back, an off licence, a Co-Op and a wet fish shop at the end, and then the 'Wishbone' restaurant.

The garage at the top of Beech Road was there and on the opposite corner was a large shop known as Central Stores. This sold groceries and cold meats.

Marie Carder: "I used to have school lunches every day except Tuesday when I went across the road to see my grandparents. We used to walk up the High Street to buy 'lunch tongue' for sandwiches at Garland's shop and then into Mrs Stile's shop, she had a newsagents and sweetshop next door."

Opposite where Tiddler's Nursery is now, was a fruit and vegetable shop owned by Mr and Mrs Young."

Marie also remembers Mattick's: "Where the library is now there used to be a hardware shop. It was long and narrow and was crammed with goods. A bell on the door announced your arrival and Mr Mattick the shop keeper would appear in a brown overall coat and would happily sell you just one or two nails or whatever it was you required."

Jill Williams remembers that to retrieve certain items that a customer might request Mr Mattick: "climbed the ladder into a loft which was like Aladdin's cave."

Marie Carder: "Next to Mattick's was the butcher's shop which was there for many years. I especially remember it at Christmas with all the ordered turkeys hanging up waiting for collection. The butcher used to sleep in the shop I believe just in case someone tried to take them. The bakers shop was at the end and was possibly my favourite, the smell of the freshly baked bread and cakes was fantastic."

Some residents also remember a shop called 'Townsend's' which was located at the end of Norman Road. According to their memories it was run by two very thin ladies and the whole of the window was full of packets and packets of cereals but it had very limited stock and really only sold biscuits.

Chapter Two – Village Characters

A car with stained glass windows, the amazing Saltford 'water-cycle' and the nicotine-fingered mid-wife with dubious beauty tips.

The village of Saltford seems to have been blessed throughout the years by a number of amazing characters, some of them eccentric others inventive and yet more of them inspired, loyal and hardworking, offering their skills and commitment to the village that they had grown up in or adopted.

One of the most colourful and best loved of these characters is Sister Touhig.

Sister Touhig

"Sister Touhig was a midwife, health visitor and district nurse rolled into one. I think it's fair to say that she was somewhat eccentric." says Cathy Hughes. "I definitely was one of her followers – if she'd advised me to do a bungee jump over the suspension bridge at nine months pregnant I would have said "'How many times?'"

"This tiny lady, hat all askew, raced around Saltford in her little red sports car," remembers Sally Smee who had her babies in Saltford in the 1960s and 1970s.

Sister Touhig's advice and instruction to generations of the ladies of Saltford began before their babies were born.

Judy Penny and Di Blatchford met in 1974 at the ante natal classes that Sister Touhig ran weekly at the Somerset Room at Saltford Hall. Di Blatchford: "Sister Touhig was a very forthright single woman (no babies) who expected us to gain only fourteen pounds in weight. I remember vividly being told to eat healthily and plenty of vitamins. One tablespoon of freshly chopped parsley had more vitamin C than a whole bottle of Ribena blackcurrant cordial."

"How could we forget the sock and tennis ball to represent the birth canal and baby's head?" Sally Smee still recalls: "'Make sure you don't lie down when you get to the hospital' she said. 'Take your pillows and insist they let you sit up to have the baby!'"

Sally still makes use of some of Sister Touhig's advice: "She taught us breathing techniques and although she had no babies of her own she said she always practiced the breathing when she went to the dentist, as I also still do!"

"If you saw her car parked on anyone's drive – it could mean a home confinement. One such day I remember when several of us mums were at the local shops with our prams and little ones – as we did most days – we saw the famous sports car parked in the Hughes' family drive in Beech Road.

'It must be Cathy,' we said, 'about to produce a new member for the Hughes family.'

Suddenly an upstairs window was flung open and cigarette in hand, Sister Touhig shouted 'It's another bloody girl!' We all shouted back our congratulations."

Cathy Hughes's own memories reveal what had actually been going on inside the house:

"One day she was in my bedroom and I was about to give birth. She looked out of the window and saw her colleague who had stopped because she'd seen the little car in our drive. Sister Touhig promptly opened the window and yelled 'Come on up – the head's just appearing!'

I didn't know who would appear – the local boy scouts maybe?! I adored this little feisty lady. I wonder what she'd make of all the rules and regulations today."

Cathy's two middle children were both born at home:

"Both times my husband and Sister Touhig were by my bedside minutes before the birth smoking – yes, smoking cigarettes like it was the last day on earth! When I voiced another contraction they both duly put their fags out in the little Tupperware dish of vinegar. When the contraction subsided, their matches and cigs were at the ready, and so it went on. When I tell my family now, the dropped bottom jaws of disbelief are a picture. I think that they think I've dreamt the whole thing up!"

Jeanne King: "Sister Touhig was a much loved figure in the village. A small wiry lady who smoked a lot. One day she rushed over to my husband to get a lift to Manor Road where a birth was imminent – her car was being serviced. My husband, David, reassured her that Dr Herapath was already there. 'That's no good,' she replied. 'He doesn't know one end of a baby from the other.'"

Once the baby was born she was full of yet more practical and timely advice.

"She wouldn't let you get dressed till the tenth day after giving birth. You had to stay in your night clothes," one lady remembered. "If you got dressed you wouldn't be treated like an invalid. Once you were up you'd not be taking it easy and doing too much."

Isobel Abernethy moved to Saltford in her early twenties with Emma who was five years old and Claire who was one year old. Isobel remembers Sister Touhig as: "being quite bossy but she was a great help to me as I was so young."

Sally Smee was relieved that Sister Touhig was not a huge advocate of bathing babies: "I remember her - much to my relief saying that I did not have to bath my screaming baby every day. 'Just top and tail' she said. 'And get the breast feeding going'."

Cathy Hughes remembers similar advice: "She was a strict advocate of breast feeding – even if only for a week because of the goodness for the little mites. Also oiling baby instead of the usual bathing for its first few weeks of life. I admit I did occasionally plonk them in the baby bath. When she visited me she used to come in the door with such a flourish that she was nearly floored by the dogs! She said that this was the difficult part of the visit but I think she secretly liked the attention."

Another of Sister Touhig's mums said that Sister Touhig would demonstrate how to oil the baby. She'd ignore the clean vest, look at the one the baby had been wearing and say 'that's not dirty' before wiping her oily fingers on it and then putting it back on the baby.

Another aid to baby health that she recommended and was not to be found on the shelves of local chemists, was the use of egg white, which she recommended putting on the baby's bottom.

And if the baby cried? "Feed, feed and feed" was her advice.

As a seemingly heavy smoker it should be no surprise that Sister Touhig's 'mums' remember her having brown nicotine stained fingers. She is also reputed to have had long nails.

Di Blatchford and Judy Penny: "After the babies were born we would attend a Thursday afternoon clinic also at Saltford Hall, run by Sister Touhig and volunteers. Our babies would be cuddled by these ladies and our moans and boasts listened to. Siblings played with toys and enjoyed juice and biscuits. Many great friendships started here. We also enjoyed buying cheaper Marmite and rose hip syrup.

We must not feed anything sweet or sweet tooth would develop."

A young dad from the time (Malcolm Pearse who was living at 526 Bath Road) also remembered Sister Touhig:

"I was in the garden working and Jonathan was in his pram outside with me when sister Touhig arrived. 'Well,' she said. 'Let's see how he's getting on.' And we went inside to weigh him. Asking where Myra was I said she had gone shopping and Sister 'T' said 'well, it's about time men took more responsibility.'"

The visit didn't go without its drama: "she put Jonathan in the net and hung it from the scales. As she was lifting it up the spring in the scales broke and Jonathan fell into her lap. 'Oh well he seems O.K.' she said. After that every time she passed me in the car with the hood down she would raise her hand as though she was going through the finishing gate at the end of a race."

Another lady recalled an incident with Sister Touhig when she visited her in her district nurse capacity. This was some time later after she'd had a benign lump removed from her breast "Sister 'T' arrived one morning to remove the stitches. "I stripped to the waist and she insisted I stood in front of the patio doors to give her more light. With no trees or bushes there for privacy I nervously pointed out that several neighbours could see me. Her reply, as I should have expected, was 'It's only a breast. They've all seen one of those before."

Marie Carder remembers Sister Touhig's nails as "being like talons" and that when one of Marie's daughters was born Sister Touhig advised: "Don't you put soap and water on that baby. Then she'll have lovely skin. I always put olive oil on my skin. I thought 'hmm', because Sister Touhig's skin was all wrinkled!"

One former Saltford 'young mum' remembers taking Sister Touhig's olive oil advice and then nearly dropping her baby because he was so slippery!

Marie also recalls that Sister Touhig professed to be able to predict the sex of the baby. In Marie's case the prediction was correct as she told Marie her baby would be another daughter and it was.

Audrey Guthrie has memories of Sister Touhig and her somewhat unusual approach to medical equipment: "She had brown tobacco stained fingers and very long nails. She would come round to do pre-natal checks on ladies who were expecting but would end up chatting and not doing the checks. She'd float in and float out and I thought 'heaven help me when I need her'. She'd sit in the kitchen smoking and drinking coffee with my mother. But once the babies came she was brilliant."

On one occasion Audrey Guthrie's daughter, Fiona had a splinter in her finger. Sister Touhig needed to use tweezers but she discovered that they "weren't in good shape." They were all twisted so she used her long brown finger nails instead. She explained that her tweezers were in the state they were because she'd used them to open a tin of soup!

Sister Touhig's former mums also remember that she would encourage them to have more babies. One of them recalls her asking: "'When are you going to have another one?' She'd keep on and on and on. I used to say I couldn't afford another one. She said 'God will provide.' She was a bundle of energy and believed in people having big families."

Another mum summed up Sister Touhig by recalling: "I can't believe it now. We were all quite feisty and intelligent ourselves but this little lady told us what to do and we did it without even thinking."

Donald Reakes

Donald Reakes moved to Saltford from Bath with his parents in 1933. They lived initially at 2, The Laurels and when the houses in Chestnut Walk were built they moved to live at number 21.

The following memories are written by his daughters: Alison Thorne and Penelope Young.

"Donald was a mechanic and together with the help of his brother Geoff they built a fully functioning car. This venture was an apparent success as they were stopped for exceeding the speed limit on Saltford Hill.

Donald also made a water cycle which he bravely (or foolishly) rode on the river, this was especially daring as he couldn't swim!

Donald worked for the village store Garland Brothers and delivered groceries around the village before the days of supermarkets. He would often do repairs for his elderly customers.

Donald had many hobbies, carpentry being his main interest. He made the case that to this day holds the bible in St Mary's Church and also the chancel table. He also had a puppet theatre and would entertain at children's parties. Characters included an elephant that squirted water, a clown, a unicyclist on a tight rope and a skeleton which appeared from a coffin and danced to the 'Dance Macabre'"

Donald's daughter Penny remembers winding up the gramophone with a handle for music to create the atmosphere for the audience.

Surprisingly Donald still had some spare time to teach violin and made musical instruments. The best known being his 'bowed psaltery' which appeared on television. He was a keen historian and would take groups of children from the school on walks around the village. "His most memorable story was the one about Frances Flood's gravestone for the burial of her feet."

Donald mended the clock on the old school and was the church warden. He helped to introduce another character to the village Reverend Stephen Wells in 1956.

Saltford resident Jeanne King remembers: "Mr Reakes was a stalwart of the church and especially the Sunday school, organising parties and outings – we even went to Weymouth on the train."

Other residents remember that during the Second World War he became a miner in Pensford and he looked after the pit ponies.

Sadly Donald died in 1983 just weeks before a service to celebrate his fifty years at St Mary's. There is a brass plaque on the bible box to mark his tremendous achievement.

Reverend Stephen Wells

Malcolm Guthrie: "In the early 1960s Stephen Wells was our rector and very involved in the school. As a dearly loved man, those of us living in the village remember one of Stephen's well known faults and that was either to forget where he had left his car ignition keys or even where he had left his car!

One day when Stephen had taken the school assembly and was about to go back to the rectory a parent, who was concerned about her child, asked Stephen for help, so they both walked gently back to the village, ignoring the rest of the world. It was only some time later, back at the rectory that Stephen remembered that his car was still parked at the school. Little did he know what a miraculous transformation to it he would find when he came to collect it!

Now, one of our greatly loved Saltford School teachers, Mike Ratnett, who lived in High Street, came up with a wonderful idea involving the school children. This plan was to decorate the windows of Stephen's car – a little Renault 4 – with coloured paper, thus creating an effect of stained glass.

When Stephen came and collected the car he thought the whole idea was absolutely wonderful – so much so that, for several days afterwards he drove around Saltford complete with stained glass windows! Eventually another much loved and respected man, Alan Christopher, who was our village constable, gently suggested that perhaps Stephen's car was not quite legal and all the stained glass was removed. The years have passed and Health and Safety now controls many of our actions but some of our little local episodes will never be forgotten."

Other Church connected characters that residents remember include:

Reverend Evans who was the rector in the 1940s. Trevor Ewins recalls: "he and his family lived in the old rectory in The Shallows. Evensong at that time was popular among the young people as it was a chance to meet socially."

Percy Sims

Trevor also recollects that one of the well-known characters connected to the church choir was: "Percy Sims, a large man who sang falsetto. Percy was a builder and in the 1930s he and his father removed the domed ceiling in the nave in preparation for the new pews. Percy was also an avid bird watcher and was very knowledgeable about wildlife around the village. In addition he organised a Christmas party for all the children."

Percy also of course produced his own volume "A History of Saltford Village". This is still available in Saltford Library.

Cecil Ewins

Cecil was the founder secretary of the Saltford Scouts Group which was formed in 1937 and was responsible for instigating the building of Saltford Hall in 1956. He was the first Chair of the Association. Cecil revived the Saltford Flower Show, which became an important event in village life. He was the organist and choir master at St Mary's Church during the war years.

The church organ must have seemed a modest affair as his son, Trevor Ewins recalled that Cecil had formerly been the organist at East Street Baptist Chapel in Bristol: "where the organ took up the whole of the east wall of the church. The air reservoir was housed in a separate room and if there was a break in the electricity it took four men to operate the pump. The organ at Saltford was much smaller and it had hand bellows which took only one person to operate."

Trevor was one of the people who would be roped in to operate the bellows. He remembers that if he'd had an argument with his dad he would sometimes let the air 'die out' and likewise if his dad wanted to make Trevor work hard he would play very loudly so that the organ needed lots of air. Bunty Dunford also remembers an occasion when she had to go and work the bellows. An event which she still remembers being so put out about at the time that she was going to leave home!

Cecil was a Special Constable in the village and a keen supporter of the Men's Club and the Women's Institute Hut.

There is a lovely stained glass window in the tower of Saltford Church, which is a memorial to Cecil. It was donated by his widow, Violet and depicts musical instruments in memory of him being the organist and choir master at St Mary's from 1940 to 1950.

Cecil died in 1973, forty years after first coming to Saltford with his wife and son. During his life time he made a huge contribution to the social life of Saltford which is still enjoyed today.

Gordon Reed

"A man with a twinkle in his eye and a mission in his heart. That was Gordon Reed," wrote Richard Davies, a reporter for the Bath Chronicle in 1994 in a biographical tribute.

Julia Chandler remembers that: "Gordon was never without a pipe in his mouth, more often than not it was not alight!

One of my fondest memories of him is when he called to change a light bulb in the very high ceiling of the main hall in Saltford Hall. First he would erect an old wooden trestle table which consisted of two or three planks of wood nested on two unfolded legs at each end. Then he would open up a step ladder and place it on top of the trestle table. He would then climb onto the extremely wobbly table and mount the step ladder in order to reach the light bulb that needed changing. And all of this with pipe firmly clamped between his teeth. Nobody ever held the ladder or wore a hard hat or goggles, that was far too cissy!"

"There is little doubt that, had he chosen somewhere else to live, he would have made a similar impact but fortune decreed that he made Saltford his home to which he gave thirty four years of unstinting service until his sudden death in 1992." Richard Davies wrote in his article for the Bath Chronicle.

Anecdote has it that Gordon was watching a cricket match, or waiting to bat himself, when he enquired about some foundations at the edge of the pitch. When Gordon was told that they were the footings for an aspirational village hall he decided that he would contribute to making this hall a reality. This new incursion of enthusiasm for the project infected many other people. He became a member of the Community Association whose prime aim was to raise funds for the hall. The next year Gordon became the Chair of the association and remained the Chair for twenty years.

It is reported that Gordon's loyalty to Saltford meant that he accepted a promotion to be the Manager of the London branch of Gresham Life Insurance only on the condition that he could continue to live in Saltford and commute by train each day.

As the 1992 Bath Chronicle notes: "Gordon could be very forthright with people with whom he did not see eye to eye or thought were not pulling their full weight, but it is difficult to imagine a man like him, who made so many things happen, not ruffling a few feathers in the process. However he made few lasting enemies and his friends can be numbered in legions."

Richard Davies also mentioned the pipe that Julia Chandler remembered so clearly and how it could be a useful tool when he was occasionally stumped by a question:

"His most constant companion was his pipe which irritated those who tried to bowl him a googly, using his favoured cricket parlance, in the form of an awkward question, because he would take a tediously long time relighting it whilst he was thinking of a suitable answer.

For Saltford he was the man of the moment. He made the village a richer place to live in. The impetus he inspired lives on today."

Drs Herapath, Harrison, Field and Gerrish

Dr Herapath, the gentleman who, according to Sister Touhig didn't know one end of a baby from the other, was another Saltford character of note in his own right. Dr Herapath, according to people who remember him, was also 'a bit of a law unto himself.' He sometimes held parties in his garden on Sunday mornings. It is reputed by certain Saltford residents, who were guests at these parties that he gave his guests drinks made from NHS orange juice and surgical spirit! These claims have not been substantiated by any evidence!

Dr Herapath conducted his surgery from his own house at the top of Beech Road opposite what is now the library. The waiting room was small and could only accommodate eight people. If there were more people than this waiting they had to queue outside in the rain.

Audrey Guthrie suggests that Mrs Herapath, his wife: "knew more about your ailments than anybody. She used to read your medical notes. She was his wife and also a nurse. If you told her anything about being ill she'd say 'yes, I know all about that."

Dr Herapath was present at the birth of one of Malcolm and Audrey Guthrie's children. The nurse escaped from the bedroom to the kitchen at one point during the labour and said: "I couldn't half do with a drink" following which Malcolm obliged by pouring sherry into two tea cups. The drink was disturbed by Dr Herapath popping is head round the kitchen door and saying "I can't see very well. Haven't you got a lamp in the garage?"

After which Malcolm retrieved the oily lamp and it was installed in the bedroom. Perhaps this allowed the doctor to discern one end of the baby from the other better. Audrey recalls that she didn't receive a cup of sherry to help with the labour herself.

Dr Herapath worked long hours. On one occasion he came out to see Bunty Dunford to give her an injection at quarter to eleven on Sunday night. When she and John apologised he just said: "Well, that's what I'm here for."

However, Dr Herapath was just one doctor in a succession of GPs, not all of them quite as well liked. Some residents' memories stretch back to Dr Harrison who was an ex-army surgeon. They recollect that he would come out of his surgery and say "You, you and you, I'll see. The rest of you can go home."

Jeanne King remembers that her husband David was very ill with blood poisoning from lead in his finger. Dr Harrison grabbed hold of his scissors and slit the patient's finger open. "If you're not better by tomorrow come back." he said. He didn't believe in antibiotics.

Dr Harrison was the GP before the NHS had been introduced: "He would charge some people and not others if he thought they couldn't manage it. These were the days of penny insurance. People paid a penny a week, which was quite a lot of money then. When the NHS came in everyone went mad and had their eyes and teeth done," recalled Pat Wood.

At the time of Dr Field and Dr Gerrish, Dr Gerrish was distinctly more popular than his colleague Dr Field.

"Everyone would rush for Dr Gerrish. One day Dr Field came into the waiting room and looked around and said: 'I am a doctor as well you know!' Dr Field would get rid of six while Dr Gerrish was seeing just one patient."

Dr Field, who had been in the RAF would look at you over his glasses and say "How are you?" and then he'd say "Hmph, you don't look too bad."

When Pat Wood was expecting her second baby and was in labour "Dr Field said: 'You've been mucking about all this time. I'm going to the races' and Dr Gerrish then came out instead."

John Dunford remembers that when he went to see Dr Gerrish because he'd lost his voice the doctor said: "Been shouting at the old trout, what!?"

Arthur Ernest Miles

Another well-known Saltford character was Arthur Ernest Miles. Arthur lived in the High Street opposite what was then the village school and was Marie Carder's grandfather. He was a stone mason by trade, he also swept chimneys and was the school caretaker, responsible for making sure the boiler was lit and the school was warm.

"My grandfather used to take me with him when he repaired walls around Saltford, many of them are still standing, and can be recognised by the distinctive pointing, done as far as I remember with an old metal bucket handle."

Roland Adams

Roland was another former Saltford resident. He grew up in the village until he was about twelve years old. His father owned land. Roland could remember getting off the train from Saltford at Green Park Station and seeing sedan chairs waiting outside to pick people up.

Ern (or Ernie) Giles

Jeanne King: "An unforgettable figure was Ern Giles, usually to be found sitting on the wall opposite Thomas's garage. He was a simple, friendly soul who liked nothing better than to wave at all the people he knew. The Thomas's were very kind to him and I believe, provided a chair in the warm in the bad weather. I think they also provided him with Christmas dinner. He was one of the last people I know to wear leather gaiters."

Mr Snailum and the cows (c. 1955)

Sheila Hall: "Mr Snailum lived with his wife at 71 High Street adjacent to the old railway bridge. He worked at Fry's until he had an accident and wasn't able to work again. He spent some of his time looking after cows that belonged to the Avery family at Spion Cop. He moved the cows to and fro into the fields owned by the Averys. There were only three or four cows; one was called Mary, a great favourite with the local children."

Billy Hill

Sheila Hall: "Billy Hill, the local lock keeper lived in the High Street. His bicycle could be seen on any passing barge as he travelled between locks. His hut is still on the Jolly Sailor Island.

Dick Hutton

Sheila Hall: "He was a council worker who kept the village neat and tidy, a cheery man."

Bill King

Bread was baked over in Corston but it was brought over to Saltford by Bill King. Bill brought it over by horse and cart. This was before 1939.

Sheila Hall: "Bill lived in Rose Cottage (almost opposite the school in High Street) which had also been his parent's home. He had a brother, Stanley who married and a sister Blanche who also married, but Bill did not marry. He worked in the Saltford Treatment Works in Mead Lane for many years until his retirement. He was a quiet man who unofficially spent a lot of time in St Mary's Churchyard attending to gravestones that were beginning to sink, and generally keeping the area tidy. He lived in Rose cottage all his life."

Chapter Three – The Railway and Transport

Hot cinders, 'Hetty the railway hen' and five shilling motor bikes

It's hard to believe now, but once upon a time there used to be two railway lines running through Saltford with a railway station for each line. One was the main line and one was the Midland Railway line.

The Midland Railway line went to Green park Station in Bath and then on to the North. The now disused line survived into the diesel age. There are still some tracks and milestones visible. It was a double track and at one time was busy. It was used by trains with two engines on the front.

The Bristolian steam train used to pass Saltford on its journey from Plymouth to Paddington.

When Sheila Hall came to live in Saltford the Kelston Station on the Midland Railway line had already closed down but she says: "the platforms stayed there for many years. Our garden backed onto the line and there was a steady incline from the bridge over Mead Lane towards Bitton which meant the engines had to get up steam. Only once in all those years did the hot cinders touch the washing on my line. A nice warm thought is the day that my clothesline prop broke – the next morning a prop was there for me at the top of the garden – courtesy of Midland Railway staff!

It was a very busy line but the highlight of the day was the Pines Express thundering through from Manchester to Bournemouth."

Sheila remembers walking along the railway line: We used to walk along the line towards Bath with family, friends and a picnic to what we called Primrose Valley, quite an adventure playground with its fallen trees, bluebell wood and primroses. The children learned that if they could feel a vibration on the rails then a train was coming, they stepped to the side and exchanged waves with the engine driver. There was no question of today's vandalism and health and safety. The children learned from an early age and this applied to the river as well."

Similarly Bunty Dunford remembers in later days there was only one train per day. She and her husband John sometimes walked along the railway line to get to Kelston woods. One day they took Bunty's Brownie pack along the line for a walk to the woods to pick bluebells to take home to their mothers. They weren't sure exactly what time the train was due to come steaming down the line so were a little worried that it might suddenly appear as they were walking along the tracks. However, they got to their destination and the train came past while they were in the woods! This one remaining train was the Bath Gasworks train.

Frances Riley has a lovely memory of Saltford Station: "I had a part-time job in Keynsham, and took the train from Saltford Station each morning.

Sometimes it was just myself and a local solicitor. We sat in the waiting room in front of a lovely coal fire. John, the Station Master or his 'oppo' would be on duty. John encouraged Hetty, a hen from a neighbouring cottage to sit before the fire. Whoever was on duty had a new-laid egg for breakfast. This event was published in a local newspaper, then in a National. But 'Oh dear' bureaucracy stepped in and Hetty had to go."

The railway was also an important feature of the village when Trevor Ewins arrived with his mother and father as a six year old in 1933: "My father worked in Bristol and like many others went to work by rail from Saltford Station. He would leave home at 8.15am and arrive at his office before 9am. Returning home, leaving Bristol at 5.15pm and home by 6pm."

For Trevor himself the railway station was an important part of exploring the village: "The Manor House and its garden and orchard were great attractions. I spent a lot of time with my dog Gypsy, a red setter, exploring the village. The playing field was the same then as now, as were the lanes such as The Batch which led to the railway station – a great place to record train numbers (a popular pastime). The LMS station was fascinating for us boys – there was a ticket office, signal levers and a waiting room but not many trains."

Margaret Stabbins was familiar with the railway in the war years: "From the age of eleven (1941) I caught the train at Saltford to Oldfield Park Station for West Twerton Senior School. The waiting room at Saltford Station was a wooden shack heated by a coke fuelled iron heater. You could see the train round the corner in the far distance and tell whether it was stopping – one lamp, or the Express – two lamps.

The trains were always late due to the wartime and I missed school assembly every day. From our house in the Shallows, it was called Willowdene, we could see on the Kelston LMS railway (now the cycle path from Bristol to Bath) the Red Cross trains going from Avonmouth, Bristol to Bath hospital, carrying the injured troops.

When the LMS railway was disbanded the rails were loaded onto flatbed wagons and removed. The big house on the hill (now lit up at night en route to Bath) was the Lord of the Manor's house (Kelston) and it is said that he gave permission to Brunel to use his land for the LMS railway which terminated at Green Park station. There was a station master at Kelston named Mr Clayfield who lived in Norman Road.

As a child of eight to ten years my sister and brother and I, when we heard the train coming faraway, we would rush to the wooden footbridge (now replaced) and feel the steam coming through just for the fun of it!" (The sister Margaret is referring to here is Bunty Dunford).

A railway tunnel runs underneath the village of Saltford. Malcolm Guthrie and his wife Audrey live in a house built over the top of the tunnel: "Having lived over the tunnel for well over fifty years I am always surprised just how many local people either don't know it's here or have no idea of its history!

It came into being when Brunel built the railway line from London Paddington to Bristol Temple Meads. Brunel of course had two other major engineering projects involving tunnels and they included the two and a half mile Box tunnel and the one and a quarter mile Severn tunnel with its major problem of breaking into the 'Great Stream' under the river Severn. This involved the installation of permanent pumps (originally steam, and now electric) to keep the tunnel dry.

Saltford Tunnel was finished quite a while before the line was opened, work being done from the Bristol and London end, which left our tunnel to be used as a workshop. Brunel used it as the assembly area for his six locos which were named Fire Ball, Spitfire, Arrow, Dart, Lyn and Meridian. Arrow and dart were built in Bristol and the others came from North Country builders. These came by sea to Bristol, dragged by horse and cart to a place near Saltford and assembled and tested in Saltford tunnel.

It must be remembered that all tunnels on this line were built to accommodate Broad Gauge (seven feet) lines which Brunel hoped would become universal but eventually Standard Gauge (four feet eight and a half inch) became almost universal across the world.

I can't confirm this but I'm told that at one time there used to be a staircase from the basement of Tunnel House down to the side of the line.

When we first moved in it used to be quite noisy when a train came through but after continuously welded lines and when steam was replaced by diesel it is now hardly noticeable."

The station was also the site of an aircraft disaster. Residents remember that two Westland Whirlwind aircraft (twin engine fighters from Charmy Down north of Bath) collided in the air whilst in a five plane formation and one came down at the railway weighbridge at the bottom of the hill narrowly missing the cottages opposite. Sadly the pilot was killed. Chris Hitching recollects that the pilot was thought to be the Squadron Commander and that the pilot

43

of the other aircraft bailed out, the pilot landing in Weston and the aircraft just south of Bath. The tragic accident disrupted the village for weeks.

Transport on two wheels

Bicycles were once a popular way of getting about the village.

Ivor Stabbins has some interesting memories about getting about on two wheels:

"When I was about twelve I had a bicycle which I was given as a present instead of going on holiday with Mum, Eileen and Dave and saving my bus and train fares towards the cost. The Raleigh bicycle was five pounds ten shillings."

He also had some old motorbikes:

"My friend Donald Hedges lived in the Grove Garage which was owned by his father. It was situated on the Bath Road just above Pixash Lane. We often tinkered with engines and built things. We once bought a motorbike between us for ten shillings (fifty pence) and repaired it. We were too young to ride it on the road so we used to keep it at 329 Bath Road.

As fuel was rationed we scrounged old dirty petrol that was used at the garage for cleaning engines, and filtered it through chamois leather. It was a bit of a long process but it meant we could get perhaps a pint of petrol which lasted us for quite a while, riding round the fields. On another occasion we decided to buy an old motorbike from

someone in Wilmington, which is near Stanton Prior. I
think we paid five shillings for it."

Chapter Four - The River, Farms and Wildlife

Eel traps, ice–skating and rowing regattas

Saltford is also fortunate in being located on the banks of the River Avon, the river which played a far more significant part in village life than it does today.

Trevor Ewins: "The river was a great attraction especially at weekends when lots of people came to hire a boat and have a picnic."

Sometimes in the winter the fields would flood and local children would skate on them. Roland Adam's father would flood his field and it would freeze. People would come from Bristol on the train and he would charge them to skate on them.

Jeanne King and Trevor Ewins both remember skating. It didn't freeze every year but when it did people would face their cars onto the ice and in the evenings the car headlights would light it up.

Children would play down by the river even if they weren't really allowed to, they would jump on top of the pontoons. One little boy got drowned. He was playing with a friend at the time and may have become tangled in weeds. The other little boy went home and didn't say anything about the accident for hours because he wasn't supposed to have been playing near the river. It wasn't until the evening that he told his mother what had happened. Everyone had been looking for the little boy for hours.

Eels used to come up the river and people used to go eeling. People ate the eels but they were never seen as a delicacy. There were eel traps and withy beds. Eels were sold at The Bird in Hand in the 1960s.

Barges used to be pulled along the tow path by horses. When the bridle path came to an end at one side of the river the horse would be transferred to the other side by a flat bottomed boat on a chain. There was one at the Jolly sailor and one at 'Granny's Steps'.

A regatta was held annually. Rowing clubs would come from all over the country. People arrived to watch by bus and train and would bring picnics with them.

Nigel Stoate who remembers the Saltford Regatta from as far back as the 1940s explains that: "the regatta in Saltford took place in recent years on the straight located between the old Clifton Rowing Club boathouse and the large meander below the Midland Railway Bridge. The old boathouse has now been demolished and replaced by three new boathouses which opened in 2014. The origins of the Saltford Regatta go back to the 1890s and continued with varying success and some wartime gaps until 1977. After this a regatta was held in Bristol Harbour.

My earliest recollections of the regatta go back to the late 1940s when I was taken there by a neighbour. After the

Second World War the event became quite an attraction and crews came to compete from Gloucestershire, the Midlands, Worcester and Hereford, South Wales and some of the Thames clubs. The event was also quite popular amongst the locals who were customers of the beer tent (open all day) before the more liberal licensing laws were brought in. A regatta dance was held in the evening for a number of years at the Territorial Army Hall by the Broadmead roundabout and in later years at Saltford Hall.

I first became involved in my early teens when much time during the school holidays was spent down by the river. We cycled, swam and played around in canoes. We used to 'help' at Sheppard's Boating Station getting the boats in and out."

Nigel became a cox and coxed for a number of years at Saltford as well as other local regattas: "About this time I was a member of Saltford Scouts and was recruited, as were some others, to become coxes for the rowing teams."

Nigel went on to cox the 'Tideway Head of the River' race which is the Oxford and Cambridge rowing course but backwards. David King also took part in this.

Nigel Stoate: "In 1957 I was lucky enough to cox a four which won trophies at Worcester, Monmouth, Saltford and the News of the World Open Sprint Championship on the Serpentine. I also rowed in a four which won at Saltford in 1962."

As Nigel himself notes, the banks of the river at Saltford has changed much over the years: "Sheppard's Boating Station and Tea Rooms has long gone and been replaced by the Riverside Inn. A Marina has been created and provides moorings for motor launches and long boats. Many of the attractive willow trees have gone, as have the cabins which were located between Sheppard's and the Rowing Club boathouses. In one of these tobacco leaves could be seen drying on the veranda."

The 'cabins' that Nigel mentions above must be the 'chalets' that Marie Carder recalled in her memories of her grandfather Arthur Ernest Miles: "He also worked in some small chalets near the towpath just past the Marina (which of course was not there then). I spent many happy hours there."

Marie also remembers walks to the river on a Sunday when she was a child:

"On Sundays we always went to Sunday school and afterwards if it was fine (it always seemed to be) we would walk to the Batch and along to the 'Outlook' and sit and gaze across to Kelston and the activity on the river."

Farms and Wildlife

Haystacks, land girls and dairy maids

Ivor Stabbins father fought in the First World War in the Somerset Light Infantry where he served in Mesopotamia and India. When he came back at the end of the war "he decided to start his own market garden. He bought some land a horse and a plough. Unfortunately the first two years were disastrous because of the adverse weather conditions and he had to sell up and look for work.

He then started working for a Miss Wills. Ivor remembers: "My childhood was very enjoyable. Dad ran a small holding for Miss Wills, who was one of the 'poor relations' of the Wills tobacco family."

This was Gwendoline Wills who residents remember being referred to by local people as 'Lady Wills'.

"It was agreed that a house would be built (Longreach Cottage) for him to rent. This meant that he had a 'tied cottage' and that he would find it difficult to leave the job he was in.

The job consisted of tilling about one and a half acres of ground for growing potatoes, cabbages, sprouts, root vegetables and any other things that could be sold to make money. In addition there were flower gardens and lawns to be tended. They kept two cows which required milking twice a day, plus sows and piglets, and approximately four hundred chickens.

Each morning dad would go into the dairy at the big house to separate the day's milk to obtain cream. The skimmed milk would then be used for the animal feeds. Some of the cream was made into butter and the surplus sold together with the eggs and vegetables etc. Some of the chickens were killed and sold dressed for the table. Dad used to drive

Miss Wills's car to deliver produce to customers around Keynsham every Friday evening.

At Christmas time the number of chickens sold was considerable which involved Dad working late in the evenings to prepare them. He received no extra wages for the hours he worked. On many occasions he would be up all night if one of the cows was calving or the sows having their litters. It was all part of the job and he had to carry on as usual the next day.

Each Saturday evening Dad would have to make up the accounts book showing what had been sold during the previous week and on Monday mornings would be called into Miss Wills's to show her these and give her the cash."

Miss Wills was a Justice of the Peace and attended Keynsham Magistrates Court each week: "This is where Dad put on his other hat and became chauffeur if she did not want to drive herself. The car always had to be cleaned and guess who did that?"

Pat Wood remembers that in the 1940s the only house at the top of Grange Road was Prior's Cott: "In those days it was only a lane and springs used to rise every winter and one had to put planks outside the gate to get over the water. What is now Keynsham Manor was a shooting box owned by a Mr Hornby who owned a farm which is now several houses. The cottage in the garden was for his gardener, a Mr Cook. One hundred cows used to be milked every day.

The milk was bottled two pints at a time in the yard opposite which was the dairy."

She recalls that the cows were kept very clean. "They were washed down with disinfectant and curry combed. Each cow was washed. If the calves had too much white on them they had to go, as they weren't pedigrees."

Pat also recalls that hay stacks were built in the field behind Grange Road.

"Roundmoor Cottage on the main road housed one of the dairy maids and another farm worker lived in what was then a small cottage on the left hand side of Manor Road.

Two land girls were employed, one of which was Violet Hill who lived on in Saltford for many years after the war. None of the Claverton Road houses were built then and it was thought that it would be impossible to build on the field as there was a lot of rock underneath and drains would have to be blasted.

There was a wonderful oak tree opposite our house in which nightingales used to sing. Blackberries could be picked along Norman Road which on one side was mainly fields."

Residents remember that at one time there were trees near the railway tracks and nightingales could be heard there too. The trees were horse chestnuts and there were also some elm trees. Some of the trees disappeared due to Dutch elm disease and others are believed to have been removed due to the leaves being a hazard on the tracks. The trees had all disappeared by the late 1990s.

At one time, residents say that peewits and plovers nested all along the banks of the river on the Jolly Sailor side and there were Great Crested Grebe in The Shallows. There were also cuckoos in the area.

Wick House Farm

People can remember buying eggs from this farm and other residents remember the farm being used to store vintage buses in the 1950s.

A Saxon or Roman coffin was once dug up in the grounds of the farm. It was unearthed when the roots of an elm tree were being removed. The remains inside the coffins were taken away but the coffins themselves remained there for a long time. Their presence unsettled some people and eventually they were also removed.

Chapter Five – Second World War

Stock-piling shopkeepers, pitch-forks and secret missions

Although Saltford didn't suffer the effects of the war in the same way as nearby city of Bristol or even the lesser bombed Bath it would have been impossible for the village to have not been affected by the Second World War.

Trevor Ewins remembers food rationing (including sweets), coupons for clothes and that most people turned their gardens into plots for growing vegetables:

"At home we took in two evacuees from London and there were several young people billeted in the village. Some of the young men from the air base at Colerne came for weekends and stayed at the 'Jolly Sailor'.

During the war most of our young people went to the pictures on Saturday mornings at the Forum or the Beau Nash in Bath and dances at the Pavilion, which attracted a lot of service men and women from the bases around the city. The Admiralty took over the Empire Hotel and built offices at Foxhill and Lansdown.

Some of the buses were converted to gas, the containers were mounted on trailers. The train was well used. The 4.38pm being popular with young people from Saltford and Keynsham who were returning from school in Bath."

Trevor joined the Royal Tank Regiment in 1944 and was sent to Germany in 1946 ending up at the Belsen Camp Unit in 1947.

Pat Wood came to Saltford during the Second World War after her family had been bombed out of Bristol: "A relative had a caravan which he placed in Trott's Farm (now Hill Farm). The farm water was provided by a well at the top of their field (which never dried out) and this was their only source of water served to a single tap in the outhouse."

Somewhat remarkably Pat's family were suspected of signalling to the German bombers from their caravan: "When the police decided we might be signalling to the German Bombers when they flew over the golf course we had to remove the caravan and managed to get a flat in what was then 11 Grange Road (now number 26). There were very few houses there then. There were two paddocks between our house and the next one. The people who lived there kept goats for the milk as one of them had T.B."

Pat also remembers that her mother: "used to sell sixpenny savings stamps in the Grange Road area and outside the library there used to be a board with a scale set up where saving totals were posted. I believe they were saving to buy a spitfire."

Ivor Stabbins remembers the war years well. At the outbreak of the war in 1939 his Uncle Roland was staying with them: "On September 1st, as it appeared likely that the war was imminent, lots of children were being evacuated from London to the West Country. The billeting officers were asking for volunteers with cars to help collect the children from the arrival points and take them to the houses were they were to stay. Roland went to Keynsham railway station and I went with him. There were about forty or fifty children, all with little bags and each with a gas mask. All had luggage labels tied to their clothing. They arrived at about five o clock. It was a sorry sight.

Although the war had not started, a blackout was in force from September 1st; the war starting on Sunday 3rd September. Roland helped to make covers with thick black paper, which was fitted up to our windows every night.

June 20th was our first Air Raid Warning but we heard no enemy aircraft. June 24th at about ten minutes to midnight we heard the air raid siren sounding. We all came downstairs and Minnie Rogers (the maid from Miss Wills's house) came to our place as she was alone at that time. Mum made us a cup of tea and then we heard the German planes and explosions as they dropped their bombs in Brislington. It seemed very near to us although it was four miles away. The all clear sounded about an hour later."

Ivor remembers that: "Friday September 27th 1940 was a lovely sunny day with no clouds. The warning sirens sounded at 11.30am and I saw ten German bombers with an escort of eighty nine fighters which were weaving above and below the bombers. They were so low that I could see the swastikas on the fuselages. Unknown to us at the time seventeen Hurricanes of 504 squadron had been sent to Filton from Hendon the previous day. The attack was planned for Parnell Aircraft Co. in Yate. Looking up it was absolutely thrilling to see the way the R.A.F. planes dived down out of the sun and within a couple of minutes all the formation was broken up and some of the German planes were destroyed. The others were chased to the South Coast. This was the last daylight raid of any size in this area."

On Sunday 24th November 1940 Ivor went with his mum and dad to the evening service at the Norman Road Chapel: "About 6.20pm the warning siren sounded and there was a lot of gunfire and all-round the hills towards Kelston there were a great number of incendiary bombs lighting up the sky. The minister said it was up to us if we wanted to go home then or wait until the service ended. I remember we stayed but when we came out to walk home there were German aircraft flying over and the sky over Bristol was very red. The raid finished about 10.50pm. During the evening about twenty High Explosive bombs fell around the Keynsham area. When the raid was over we didn't hear the All Clear Siren as we had lost the electricity supply. J.S. Fry had a steam driven hooter which they normally used to give the start and stop signal to their factory so that was used to give the All Clear. It was three or four days before the electricity was on again."

Chris Hitching recalls that "On D Day, 6th June 1944 many of the troop carrying Dakotas of both the British and American forces came over Saltford at a low level and with their navigation lights on – quite a site."

And that "During the summer of 1943 we had an insight into the build up to D Day when on a sunny day we had a convoy of one hundred and thirty plus Sherman tanks coming through Saltford from Avon mouth heading to the Warminster area."

A few days after his fifteenth birthday Ivor Stabbins joined the Local Defence League. The following is Ivor's account of his experiences as a member:

"No doubt most of you have watched 'Dad's Army' on the television and wondered how much of it was based on fact. A little history may help you to decide:

By May 1940 the government decided that civilians should be asked to enrol to form a force that could help repel the Germans who were expected to invade the British Isles. Volunteers were asked to join at their local police station. My father joined up almost straight away. The recruits had no weapons issued, some owned a shotgun, but the majority had nothing to use except a pitchfork.

Eventually an arm band was issued with the letters L.D.V. (Local Defence Volunteers). Many people said it stood for 'Look, Duck and Vanish'! It was about six months before uniforms were received and the LDV became the Home Guard. About this time some rifles were sent to them from the USA.

The recruiting age was seventeen years old but as I wanted to take part in the training, a few days after my fifteenth birthday I told the enrolment officer that I was 17 and was accepted. So much for the history. The training consisted of rifle drill and firing at targets. We had lectures one night per week in Keynsham Drill Hall. In addition every Sunday morning we carried out field exercises at different places outdoors and manoeuvres, sometimes against other platoons as rivals. Our main night duty was to patrol an area at Burnett. Our unit consisted of a lieutenant, a second lieutenant, two sergeants, corporals and other ranks. Our leader was the lieutenant (who I think we will call 'Mainwairing').

We did not have a butcher who could supply the transport when required but our Mr Mainwairing had access to the director of Keynsham Paper Mill for whom he worked. One of the workers was a lorry driver and also a member of our platoon. The transport consisted of a driver's cab and an open trailer which could carry a large number of men and supplies required for our platoon.

Not long after I enrolled a few of us were training in how to use hand grenades which I expect you know are thrown into crowds and explode about five seconds after it leaves the hand of the thrower. I was not very keen on any sport at school (which included cricket). One of our sergeants took a few of us to an isolated field bounded by a loose stone wall. After watching the other fellows throw their grenades it was my turn. The object was to stand about ten yards in front of the wall and lob it over. To prepare it for exploding, you pulled out a pin as it left your hand. My grenade didn't get far enough over the wall. The sergeant with me yelled out to lie as flat as possible and it was immediately followed by the metal pieces flying over our heads. It was lucky that the sergeant was with me. Mr Mainwairing would have said 'stupid boy', which I was.

We also had to take our turn at Burnett for night duty. This site was virtually on the road which overlooks Saltford and leads to Corston. Behind us was an underground ammunitions dump which was part of the reason for our presence. Our patrols consisted of six men working in pairs for a three hour shift. When your three hours were up you returned to a wooden hut which held the off-duty men. There was always a sergeant or corporal in charge of communications. The hut had no electricity or water, so paraffin was used was used for lighting and boiling water to make a cup of tea which was welcome when you had come in after a three hour patrol. The lorry which took us to Burnett also carried two five gallon drums, one with water in and the other with paraffin so we could manage through the night. I was on the nine till midnight shift with another colleague and as we finished we went into our hut. As soon as I went in it was nice to see the kettle boiling. We were handed our teas, my first comment was 'it smells of paraffin!' then 'it is paraffin!' The kettle was still boiling on the stove so I took it off quickly realising that this was a dangerous vapour which could have burst into flames. Normally the hut had a paraffin smell but this was too much. I never found out who was responsible but the drums were carefully labelled after that. We were very lucky that the whole hut wasn't ablaze.

Sunday mornings were normally used for outside activities. On this occasion it was to capture a rival platoon. The distance between us was probably about a mile but in order to contact them they knew we had to cross the River Chew. This was very shallow in one area so would be easy to wade across. Our rivals would be waiting for us on the other side. Lieutenant Mainwairing was one step ahead and decided that we should cross the river where it was quite deep but only about ten feet wide. With his forward planning we had a wooden bridge made probably at Keynsham Paper Mills. It was approximately fourteen feet long but not very wide. Our transport brought it down and somehow it was dropped into position to span the water. When our platoon arrived the temporary bridge was ready to cross. Lieutenant Mainwairing led his men to the edge of the river and shouted 'Follow me men!' and started to cross the bridge until halfway across he fell into the river. He was helped out, shivering, as it was a very frosty morning. Later that morning Mainwairing arrived back in his civilian clothes.

Well, that's it. I feel that the three examples I mentioned were not unusual, but our training was helped by all the officers and senior staff making us into very competent soldiers who would have been able to defend this country while our troops were fighting overseas.

Stick to watching 'Dad's Army' it is a bit over the top and excellent entertainment. Just one more shot, our platoon was allocated a Browning automatic rifle. I was put in charge of it instead of the normal rifle, which was far better than grenade throwing."

As well as the usual 'Dad's Army' there is evidence that Saltford was also a base for a Special Brigade. Some years after the war, Malcolm Guthrie was once taken by a friend to Longwood in Saltford. The friend showed him a place with a brick entrance and a rusty door. Malcolm's friend told him that if the Nazis had invaded this was all set up to be an operation centre of a special resistance group. The centre had been filled in by the time Malcolm saw it. He told him that Churchill was behind the organising of these groups and there would have been three in the South of England. Saltford was one of them and the other two were in the Hastings and Portsmouth areas. These areas had Special Brigades waiting to act. The father of Malcolm's friend had been a member of the special command.

The Saltford Scouts also played their part in the war. During the course of the war fifty or sixty incendiary bombs were dropped in the field behind the Manor House, Trevor Ewins remembers. Some of them quite close to the house itself. Trevor still has a letter from Noel Flowers (the owner of the house at the time) written to his father Cecil Ewins, praising the Scouts for putting out the incendiary bomb fires.

Noel Flowers wrote: *"Destruction is wholesale and we know it must continue...mercifully, England's courage is Indestructible. So far as my personal experience goes, everyone seems to take a pride in showing how much they can stick. Certain it is, unless Britain wins through each one of us would be better dead."*

And of the Scouts themselves he wrote: *"What a splendid Record ... 50 Incendiaries put out by 2 Scouts in the Home Field and Yard. I admire the boy's performance so greatly that I feel a reflected pride that their Good Deed should have happened on my property. Well battled the Scouts!"*

Another less exemplary story of Saltford during the war relates to Miss Mitchell who owned the sweet shop in the An incendiary bomb actually came through her roof and landed on her bed. This is believed to be the only property actually seriously damaged during the whole course of the war.

The Wilson family next door had a relative staying who, story has it, gained access to Miss Mitchell's house, rolled up the bomb in a mattress and threw it out of the bedroom window.

It is alleged that Miss Mitchell had been stock piling sugar, waiting for prices to go up. She had packets of it stored all the way up her staircase. Her guilty secret was exposed by this incident. All her stockpiled goods were destroyed by the damage and by the firemen hosing the house out with water.

Chris Hitching also remembers that it was maintained that Miss Mitchell had stored cigarettes in her bedroom under the bed and that because of this that part of the house was particularly badly damaged.

Bunty Dunford recalls passing Miss Mitchell's shop on the way to school the following morning and seeing the still smouldering mattress and thinking 'poor Miss Mitchell'.

Chris Hitching remembers that "two petrol stations were involved in storing four Hawker Typhoon fighters each. The garages were the Crown Garage (owned by Mr

Bendall) and St Keyna Garage known as Norman Garage (owned by Mr Mattick)."

Chris also recalls that "On a Sunday in 1943, ninety eight Lancaster bombers passed over an area between Keynsham and Bath, with Saltford getting its fair share. These aircraft were at a height of one hundred to two hundred feet. So low were they that after coming over Lansdown they could not be seen from the top of Beech Road until they shot out of the Avon valley and up over Saltford. The high poplar trees in our garden were shaking in the slipstream. I have since found out that they flew at this height all the way to Le Creuset in France (via the bay of Biscay) to bomb a factory. I believe that on this mission they lost two aircraft."

But what were past and contemporary Saltford residents who were in the services doing during the war?

Dick Bateman spoke to Malcolm Guthrie about his war time experiences and the following is his tribute to Malcolm: "In the Second World War Malcolm was an RAF bomber flight engineer and second pilot in Halifax bombers from airfields in eastern England.

As we walked up Kelston Round Hill together he told me that if he had joined his squadron six months earlier his chances of survival would have been vastly reduced. A change in the pattern of bomber flights, however, meant that his group of aircrew, though in great peril every flight, stood a much better chance of getting back in one piece than their predecessors.

As Hitler's intentions to invade Poland had become clear before the war, the Czech government decided that Hitler should not have their gold. They sent the bullion by rail to Marseilles, where it was loaded onto a British warship and taken to London, where it was kept safe in the bank of England until Hitler was defeated and the Czechs asked for it back.

After the war Malcolm's plane and another Halifax bomber were given a secret mission. As Loading Officer, Malcolm was ordered to load up top secret cargo from London. It became clear that Malcolm's plane was to take half the pre-war Czechoslovak gold reserves back to Prague.

They were told that they would be met by high ranking Czech authorities when they arrived in Prague. The two planes took off from RAF Northolt together, but became separated. Malcolm's plane eventually landed near Prague and his cargo was removed, not by the Czechs but by Russians.

So far so good – but Malcolm's friend, the other pilot, did not land in Prague, though that was his destination. Neither he, nor the plane and its cargo were ever seen again... Malcolm has no idea what happened to the pilot, crew or the gold.

Malcolm himself has related a number of other war time memories:

"I was working in London when I joined the RAF. I saw an advertisement at the bottom of the Strand saying 'Exchange your overalls for a flying kit'. I made the first real decision of my life and I spent the morning joining up to be air crew with the RAF. When I got home and told my mum she burst into tears but she was sure that I would fail the medical. I didn't."

Malcolm trained to be a pilot but, at the beginning of the war, there were actually too many pilots. He didn't want to be a glider pilot so he re-trained as a flight engineer. He was in 296 Squadron which was part of Special Forces:

"The crossing of the Rhine was the biggest obstacle to the Allies. Eisenhower wanted twenty thousand men dropped on the German side of the Rhine with the object of securing three bridges."

The operation to do so was called Operation Varsity and Malcolm took part in it. Over three thousand aircraft crossed the channel early that morning. Malcolm's aircraft was carrying fifteen paratroopers. As engineer Malcolm carried responsibility for the aircraft: "Everything was checked and checked again before the operation. We flew over to the Dover/ Folkestone area with a specific order on how to join up with the rest of the stream of aircraft. It was the biggest concentration of aircraft all up in the air together ever. I took a photo with a box Brownie camera but the planes just looked like dots."

The route had a diversionary 'dog leg' to give the German's a false impression of their destination. When they ran into their first anti-aircraft fire it was 'heavy and accurate': "shrapnel hit the aircraft casing. There would be a buffeting from explosions but it was usually soundless as we couldn't hear anything except engine noise. Sometimes we would hear a clattering or tinkling sound of fragments. There were a fair number of casualties. The squadron had twenty aircraft, three didn't return, two got taken prisoner."

After the release of the gliders at their destination: "the plane itself flew in a full dive and then set course to get home as quickly as possible. We flew back with another Halifax aircraft from our squadron. We were flying no more than thirty or forty feet up. We saw a farmer with a herd of cows. The farmer was sitting on a stool milking. The cows were so startled by the noise of the low flying aircraft that the cow gave a tremendous kick sending the farmer flying.

We crossed the coast at Clacton. We landed and had a normal de-briefing. We had a second breakfast at 10am. The aircraft was checked over and we took on ammunition, 500lb bombs, and were carrying out another operation by midday. This was a supply drop to people on the ground. We got back mid-afternoon and had a third breakfast! We carried out a further supply drop that night. Supplies were dropped in wicker baskets on parachutes."

After the war lots of prisoners that had been held in German concentration camps were brought back to Belgium by train: "Brussels airport was a collection point for hundreds and hundreds of concentration camp refugees." The Halifax aircraft were turned into troop carriers in a matter of days. Wooden seats were installed.

Malcolm's plane landed in Belgium and they were given lists of people, who were marshalled by the army, to transport. Malcolm's plane took twenty five women from Auschwitz and Treblinka. They were all Greek and Malcolm's plane flew them home:

"When we landed in Lucca, Italy the number of passengers had increased to twenty six. One of the women had given birth!"

Chapter Six – Childhood, School and Scouts

Dame schools, gas lamps and Waltzing Matilda

Given the tremendous changes that have taken place over the last few decades it would be surprising if the experience of present day children were the same as those of yesterday.

Trevor Ewins went to school in Saltford in the 1930s: "I walked to school down Beech Road past Poles Corner filling station with its hand operated petrol pumps. There was a stream running down the left hand side and a circle of trees in the middle of the field on the right hand side. The war memorial was at the junction of the High Street and Norman Road. The old village was clustered around the school and the Manor House."

Once at school Trevor remembers that: "There was a house adjoining the school in the playground. The school consisted of three classrooms, two in the main part of the building and one in the Kelly Room to the left of the building and accessed from the cloakroom. Mrs Bunker was the Headmistress. As well as learning the three 'R's the rector made us learn the catechisms. Every morning we had a break for a small bottle of milk. After school we went to Miss Mitchell's sweet shop and played in the surrounding fields."

When Ivor Stabbins was five years old he travelled from Saltford to Keynsham to go to school where he attended Keynsham Infants in Temple Street: "Eileen, my sister and I walked to Keynsham each morning and we had a penny each for the return journey, which was the bus fare to Saltford. In fact we usually walked home to save the penny. Eileen was at Bath Hill School and finished later than the infants school, so I would normally wait for her to come out and then walk home with her. On one occasion I remember walking on my own. A motorist stopped his car to ask if I was lost. Obviously I knew where I was going and carried on."

However when Ivor was seven he left that school and started at Redcliffe Endowed Boy's School in Bristol "Originally I used to catch the bus to Keynsham Church, then meet Ron Ford at Keynsham railway station. We then caught the 8.11am train to Bristol Temple Meads. We then walked from the station to Redcliffe."

David Cox was born in Beech Road 13th November 1942: "I became immediately aware that this would put me into a lower academic year than I would have liked! Secondly that there was a war on, which was inconvenient since it meant that toys were in short supply and often second hand! I remember with great affection my pedal car and later my trike.

As time went by the word 'school' seemed to occupy my parents' conversation which I found somewhat alarming since I could find no fault with the status quo.

Eventually the dreaded day arrived. I was still two months short of my fifth birthday. We sauntered down through the village. But in their wisdom my parents decided to shun the village school, so turned right opposite the said building up the Batch. In those days the last house on the right was being used as a 'dame school' run by a Mr and Mrs Percival, a kindly but strict couple whose academic standards were considered to be somewhat higher than those enjoyed at the village school.

However the curriculum was broad including art and craft, music and Physical Education all taught in an upstairs room, heated in winter by a paraffin bowl fire which worked rather like a primus stove. Lighting was by gas lamps since mains electricity was late coming to that part of the village.

Religious Education played no part in this curriculum but our moral welfare was not neglected. Honesty was high on the list of priorities. One incident I remember to this day occurred when one of my peers told a lie which he refused to own up to. He was warned of the consequences but bravely (or foolishly) wouldn't budge, so Mr Percival collected the tablet of soap from the toilet and in front of the assembled school washed his mouth out with it. Needless to say we were all horrified but suitably chastened."

Trevor Ewins was at King Edward's School in Bath during the Second World War. He travelled from Saltford to Broad Street each day. He recounted: "It was a five storey building. When the air raid sounded we had to go down all the stairs to the vaults in Broad Street which were used as shelters. Our Master was Mr Morgan and he was deaf. If we got to a difficult part of the lesson someone would shout 'Siren, sir!' and then we would run all the way down and have to come back up again."

Trevor also remembers that as pupils of the school they were sent to the Guildhall to help record deaths from air raids and people's whereabouts in Bristol.

He recalls wearing short trousers and a cap. They even had to wear the cap when they were out of school in town. If they didn't and were seen without it they would be told off by the master.

A number of Saltford residents remember getting the cane at school and John Dunford recollects getting pages and pages of 'lines': "I must not run in the corridor. Pages and pages of them." He tried the experimental approach of using more than one pen at the same time!

At first the village school at Saltford down High Street was both an infant and junior school. Then as the number of children increased the infant school moved to Ellsbridge House. This was from about 1953. Children continued to use Ellsbridge House until a new school opened down Claverton Road.

Marie Carder's memories are from the 1950s onwards: "I remember getting on a coach every morning by the Memorial Park and being taken with all the other five and six year olds to Infant School in Ellsbridge House. The entrance road seemed very long and we sometimes went for nature walks to find flowers around the drive. When we were seven we progressed to the Junior School which was in Saltford Village."

Mrs Hutchcroft was the Head Teacher at one time, a Saltford resident remembers. Mrs Hutchcroft was made an O.B.E. For a while she left the school and went to be an Education Advisor in Peru. Then she returned from Peru and resumed her Headship. Saltford residents report that after that she would 'float around in a poncho'.

Other Head Teachers at the school included: Mrs Bunker, Mrs Drewitt (who lived at The Outlook – a wooden building on Cox's Close) and Miss Frasier. At one time the Head Teacher lived in a little cottage that was joined onto the school buildings at the back. This was later demolished.

School lessons were held in the hall. Lunches were delivered in tin cans which some former pupils recall as being 'horrible'. Milk for the children was also delivered and would be warmed up on a little stove.

Childhood out of school hours

Ivor Stabbins remembers that in the school summer holidays he and his sister and mother would go away on holiday: "Although Dad could not get away from the work, Mum always took Eileen and I for a week's holiday, usually accompanied by Auntie Olive. Quite often it was to Weston-Super-Mare where we would have 'Rooms and Attendance'. This was bedrooms and a room downstairs where we would have breakfast and our evening meal. We would supply our own food and the landlady did the cooking and cleaned up. One particular place where we were, Eileen and I used to dread this landlady coming in to clear the breakfast things and staying chatting to Mum when we were anxious to get down to the sands. We went to Southsea or Bournemouth and sometimes Ron Ford went with us."

Chris Hitching was born down Beech Road in 1930. He and his brother Peter "were involved with other children in the village playing cricket and football in the field behind the church (where I was christened)."

His brother Peter and sister Jennifer were also born in the village.

He remembers that he and the other children: "used to play Kick Tin in the humpty dumps on the Kelston side of the river. At times we roller skated down the High Street, past The Bird in Hand, down the hill under the railway bridge to Mead Lane and Avon Lane, possibly causing a little annoyance to the older residents of the High Street."

During the summer they also helped out at Sheppard's Boathouse "launching and retrieving the skiffs used in short rentals on the river. In the evenings we used a three-scull boat to collect any of the boats that were still out, and boats hired by the American servicemen who couldn't be bothered to return them."

Myrna Jones went to ballet classes in Saltford when she was a child in the village:

"When I started ballet lessons over sixty years ago, classes were held in the Bird in Hand. They were held in a green corrugated building on the side of the pub. Soon afterwards lessons were held in the W.I hut in Norman Road. I enjoyed doing many dancing displays there. In my dance class was a then young girl called Penny Nice. Later she was the hostess for 'Mr and Mrs' on the T.V."

The Boy Scouts

The Boy Scouts have played an important and integral part in village life throughout the decades in Saltford. They cleared incendiary bombs from the fields behind the Manor House and formed a messenger group based in the Men's Club to relay messages when the phone lines broke down during the Second World War. They also guarded the Saltford Carnival Flower tent from any attempts at subterfuge by over- competitive entrants!

Cecil Ewins was the Scout Master in 1939 and under his leadership the Scouts moved to the Manor House in Saltford. The owners, the Flower Family were not living in the house and it had fallen into disrepair. Trevor Ewins said "Father wrote to the owner, a certain Mr Lamrock Flower, who lived in Devon".

Trevor remembers what a wonderful place it was as a Scout Headquarters with the orchard and fields to camp in.

There is an original document still in existence from 1940 which publicises a 'Camp Fire and Sing Song', admission was threepence. It also refers to the 'earliest known window seat'. This window seat is in one of the bedrooms at the Manor House and was re-discovered by some of the scouts who pulled away some plaster and found the ancient seat behind it.

Boy Scouts Association

1st SALTFORD GROUP

KEYNSHAM ASSOCIATION

Opening of
New Headquarters

at

THE MANOR FARM, SALTFORD

(Kindly loaned by Noel Flower, Esq.)

January 7th, 1939

ADMISSION BY PROGRAMME

PRICE 6d. (including refreshments)

Scouts in Uniform Free

A new "Illustrated History of Saltford Manor" is now on
Sale, price 6d. All profits in aid of Saltford Scout Funds.

David Cox: "In November 1951 I was enrolled in the Wolf Cub Pack under the leadership of William Cecil Harrison (usually known as Cecil but in scouting circles known as 'Bill') who had been Akela (leader of the pack) for 6 years by then."

The formation of the 1st Group in Saltford had taken place in 1927 under the leadership of Mr Exon. The neckerchief at that time was red and blue.

In the 1920s the Saltford Scouts took part in a World Jamboree at Arrowe Park. Two of the Saltford Scouts entered the Somerset Boxing Championship and both won. A team from the Saltford Group also won the Somerset Swimming Championship.

In 1940 the War Service Scout Patrol was formed working with Air Warden Services. This was at the time that Trevor Ewins was a Cub Leader.

On 25th June 1960 the Scouts new headquarters were opened by the County Commissioner but in October 1961 they were completed destroyed by fire. The scouts carried on in temporary accommodation loaned by the Women's Institute and Saltford Men's Club. An opening of a new HQ took place in 1964.

In 1979 as part of the celebrations to mark the golden anniversary of the first formation of the group an open day with an evening dinner at the Saltford Community

Association was held and was followed by a 'Gang Show'. The Gang Show then became a regular event every three years.

David Cox (Group Scout Leader 1980 – 1999): "Over the years the number of boys has increased considerably so that from 1970s onward there were two Cub packs and two Scout troops and a Venture Unit for the over fifteens. Also included was a Beaver pack for the six to seven year olds. A further alteration was the admission of girls to all sections."

During the 1960s the boys found themselves featuring in films produced by the Bristol Cinematic Society.

In 1982 the Saltford Scouts undertook a sponsored washing machine push from Saltford to Baden Powell House in London, raising over one thousand pounds for Scout funds!

An institution of the Scout movement is of course the annual camp.

Jeanne King: "Another great occasion of the year was the Scout Camp. A favourite campsite was the river Usk in Llangynidr, where the boys would swim. I think health and safety rules would now put a stop to some of the activities and games. But it made an exciting and confidence building time. Everyone came home tired, grubby and smelling of wood smoke.

The boys were fortunate in having young leaders with lots of energy such as Trevor Ewins, Pete Timney and my husband, David King who later became 'Skip' after 'Bill' Harrison retired and younger ones like David Cox."

David Cox himself remembers his introduction to the Saltford Scouts:

"Once I had joined the Scouts more activities became available to me including fire lighting, First Aid, knots and pioneering projects, how to pitch a tent properly – all the skills needed for camping. Each summer the whole troop would pack all our camping kit into the back of a Tate and Lyle lorry. Mr Hoddinott would drive it, with us on board, to our chosen camp site where we would unload it before eating our packed lunches, after which it would be time to put up our tents and lay out our kitchens – one for each patrol. The next task was to dig a fire pit, a wet pit and a dry pit for kitchen waste. Every patrol was responsible for its own cooking.

The Seniors (later to be called the Venture Scouts) were responsible for the toilets. These consisted of an enclosure of six foot high hessian surrounding a pit about two feet square with a layer of small stones for drainage and a six foot long trench which one had to squat over – a frightening experience for first timers!

On the last evening we always had a campfire where we sang all the old favourite songs such as 'Ging Gang Goolie', 'Clementine' and 'Waltzing Matilda' plus any new ones that anyone had to offer and was prepared to lead.

All the years I was in the 1st Saltford Group the centre piece of any camp or open event was Oscar. Now Oscar had originally been fashioned by William Cecil Harrison from a section of tree trunk to form a totem pole. It was much prized by us boys and unfortunately at jamborees, by boys from other troops who did their best to kidnap it! Later on Oscar was copied onto our Group Badge, which is now found on every neckerchief in the group."

Girl Guides

Diane Hooper, who is the President of Saltford Guiding says:

"Girl Guiding began in Saltford in about 1940. Some interested Guides began meeting in the upper room of The Crown pub. The father of Miss Radcliffe did not feel it was a fitting place for young ladies to be meeting! On the occasion of his daughter's twenty first birthday he presented her with a plot of land in Lansdown Road, on which a small hut was erected. Thus a more suitable venue was provided.

Many older members could remember meeting there, such as Lilith Reakes, Nora Cheal, Peggy Shellards, Dorothy Cook, Olive Brown and Audrey Stook, all of whom became loyal members of the community.

The old hut was eventually replaced with an ex-school terrapin hut built on stilts about three feet off the ground. This proved to be a very noisy building and a Saltford resident still alive today remembers being asked to bring slippers to wear to try and eliminate the problem!"

This building also started to deteriorate. When the roof began to leak a building committee was formed. The 'Trefoil Guild' formed in 1987, was made up of former guides. All means of fund raising were adopted. Alongside more traditional methods such as sponsored cycling and coffee mornings they invested in Premium Bonds and even put money on the horses after studying racing form! Unfortunately the horses didn't win! However eventually forty thousand pounds was raised, plans were drawn and approved "and the Guiders celebrated the end of an era with champagne." Would Miss Radcliffe's father have approved of all this betting and alcohol?

Ann Mallard remembers: "The 2nd Saltford Guides decided to celebrate with a midnight hike to Kelston and a sleep over at the old hut. One of our dads was coming early the next morning for demolition."

The girls decided to cover the walls in graffiti: "It was an incredible work of art – it contained their memories. I hadn't realised we had done so much."

When demolition started there was "a big mix of emotions, really sad, I think tears were shed, but it was also exciting as we were now looking forward to a new era."

Diane Hooper "The interior was fitted out by many local tradespeople. Dads worked under the supervision of the local craftsmen. A rota of mums and Guiders kept the men supplied with tea and biscuits, an essential part of any work party. Eventually the hut was finished and the stone wall was rebuilt by two local scouts!"

Chapter Seven – Village Buildings

Sing songs at the Manor House, ancient light bulbs, and a lady named 'Fluff'

What makes up a village? Is it people or buildings? Well of course it is both and both affect each other. As village characters have come and gone (but perhaps passed on their characteristics to new generations of their family) the buildings of the village have also altered in some ways and new waves of buildings have appeared. Saltford still has some ancient buildings in the High Street that date back for centuries. Village buildings include all the variety you might expect in a village that dates back centuries: cottages, grander houses, village school, church, pubs, garages, a war memorial and some buildings that have changed their purpose a number of times over the years.

The Manor House

The Manor House is on Queen's Square. The house was called Saltford Farm and not Saltford Manor until relatively recently. It was owned by the Flower family. The Manor House had a private chapel at one time but this has now been demolished.

Before regular refuse collections were established local people used to bury their rubbish in the vicinity of the Manor's old fishponds in which, many years before, carp had been bred.

The Flower family have not been inhabitants of the village for many years but some descendants of the family, a brother and sister who lived in Bath, turned up at the church one day when Bunty Dunford was taking her turn in an annual vigil that used to be held. They were interested in finding out about their ancestors.

There is a belief, still held in Saltford, that at one time there were two manor houses. This belief derives from the fact that there is a bill of sale from the 1600s relating to a second Manor house.

High Street

Some local people remember when High Street had a serious incident of subsidence and the road collapsed just outside what is now the Church Hall. Due to the collapse of the road an 'ancient oak-beamed tunnel' was discovered which was thought to be a medieval drain. Resident Malcolm Guthrie knows this first hand as he and a friend went in to explore.

Saltford Mill

"It would be reasonable to suggest," says Julia Scott, the daughter of Hugh Folliott, who purchased the mill in 1963,

"that the Saltford Mill at the end of Mead lane and next to the Jolly sailor Inn would have a recorded history going back for hundreds of years but there seem to be no records about it."

There were a number of mills in the area and nobody is quite sure which is the old mill. However this mill is likely to be the oldest one. It was originally a tucking mill, with the purpose of cleaning wool.

Trevor Ewins: "It was the paintworks when I first knew it in the 1940s. It was owned by the Tailor family. Lorries brought in the raw materials through the village and then Lorries would transport the finished paint product out again through the village."

But how did Hugh Folliott become involved in the mill? Hugh Folliott was an inventor, his inventions included an automatic toaster. Julia Scott, his daughter remembers growing up in a house where toast was popping up all over the place as her father tested various timers on different models! The patent was eventually sold to Kenwood.

He bought the old Saltford Mill in 1963. It was a "ramshackle building, says Julia Scott, "almost an industrial museum with a leaking, corrugated roof at the time. It leaked everywhere and was drafty and cold. However there were excellent views of the river and from its windows river traffic and kingfishers could be observed. The fields were across the river – and the pub was next door – so there were compensations!"

The compost that was produced from this building was called Vermipeat and the company also went by this name. Hugh had invented a formula for a soil-less compost, which incorporated a substance known as 'vermiculite'. This was probably the first soil-less compost to be produced in Britain. After producing this compost Hugh went on to invent what he called 'Readipots'. The 'Readipots' were solid blocks of Vermipeat bonded into the shape of a plant pot and then shrink wrapped in polythene. Although shrink wrapping went on to be a universal method of packaging, Hugh Folliott's use of this technique was well ahead of its time.

As Julia remarks "It was a top flight product, not properly marketed as Hugh's forte was inventing and not the running of a business. Nonetheless the product was acclaimed by horticulturalists all around the world. It continued production for more than twenty years and employed up to twenty five people.

Wally Barnes was the factory manager, who with little complaint, coped with the fairly Heath Robinson hand to mouth existence of the factory."

For some time the product was in demand and the Bristol Evening Post on March 1st 1967 noted "from Trinidad and Barbados to Greenland and Israel". It was used for the production of such varied crops as Channel Island tomatoes, African sugar cane and Malayan rubber plants.

Hugh died in 1969. After his death Julia and her husband took the business on. (Julia's husband, John was also the Chair of the first Saltford Parish Council after being one of the people to set the council up from the Saltford Residents' Association).

Eventually bigger companies produced similar products of their own and the mill was eventually sold in 1984 to Saltford pottery and it is now converted into industrial units.

Saltford House

This house is sometimes mistakenly thought to be the Manor House, even in some earlier publications.

At one time it was used as a residential home for nurses working at Keynsham Hospital. It was still occupied by nursing staff in 1957. Later on it was used as offices and then was unoccupied. At this stage it became occupied informally for a time by what Malcolm Guthrie described as 'a lovely bunch of squatters' who were very polite and invited neighbours in for tea!

Before being a residential home for nurses it had been owned by the Coles family. Malcolm Guthrie also recalls that there used to be a cast iron canopy that was covered in wisteria but all this was demolished. However some of the wisteria survives as Malcolm took a cutting from the original before it was destroyed and planted it in his own garden. Later when Ivor Ford bought Saltford House Malcolm told him about the lovely wisteria from which he'd taken a cutting years before. This was now thriving in Malcolm's garden and in turn Malcolm gave Ivor a cutting so the beautiful wisteria was restored to the gardens of Saltford House.

Tunnel House

An ancient light bulb was discovered in Tunnel House which was compatible with an old two hundred and ten volt system. The bulb has a receptacle at the top through which it's believed that nitrogen would have been injected. Malcolm Guthrie believes it must have been over a hundred years old, however when he took it home and tested it he discovered that it still worked!

Norman House

Norman House is an ancient dwelling and is located on the High Street. It was previously a farm and people used to collect milk from it.

Sheppard's Boat House

There were two boathouses. They were both owned by the Sheppard's and both eventually burnt down. Those local people that remember them recall that they were made out of wood but had red corrugated roofs. One of the boathouses had a tea room on top which sold tea and cakes. A lady known as 'Fluff' apparently served tea there. Those that remember her say that she was also an usherette in a cinema. There were wooden stairs to get up to the tea room and boats were kept underneath. In between the two boathouses was a little kiosk that sold ice-cream.

After the Second World War some landing crafts (L.C.A.s – landing craft – assault) were stored near the boathouse. They were stacked one on top of the other. It's believed that during the war they had been in Bristol docks waiting for redeployment at D day but they were not used and the reason they were later in Saltford was because someone had the idea that they could convert them into houseboats.

Cottages

There are a number of centuries old cottages on the High Street in Saltford. Marie Carder remembers her grandparent's cottage: "It was quite small but very cosy and warm. There was no running water inside and cooking was done on a gas cooker but also in ovens at the side of the open fire. There was no electricity and I remember peering through the gloom waiting for them to decide if it was dark enough to light the gas mantle!

I loved their garden which sloped upwards and was full of flowers and a large bird bath."

Brass Knocker

"The Post Office was not always where it is now," one Saltford resident remembers. "When I was a school child (about seventy five years ago). It was in the village at the bottom of the Batch in the house known as the Brassknocker." It was the first telephone exchange in the village and was manually operated.

Telephone numbers were very short some Saltford residents remember. You would phone the operator and say "can you connect me to" whoever you wanted to phone. Mrs Highman was the operator and sometimes she would say "they're not in today" if she happened to know the person you wanted to speak to had gone out! This was in the 1940s.

The Crown Garage

The garage was run by a Mr Bendle who sold Moskowitz cars imported from Russia and R.O.P. which stood for Russian Oil Petrol but which local people used to refer to as 'Rotten Old Petrol'! It's believed that Mr Bendle probably sold these rather eccentric products because they were cheap.

The War Memorial

At one time there were two gangs of local children in Saltford the 'top gang' and the 'bottom gang'. The war memorial marked the divide between the two gangs.

The war memorial used to be in the middle of Beech Road. Beech Road originally had a stream running down it and the children would paddle in it on their way home from school. There were primroses on the banks of the stream. Some residents of the village remember a cart once getting stuck in the stream.

The positioning of the war memorial in the middle of the road confused many drivers as they weren't sure which way to go round it and there would often be a squealing of brakes as drivers slowed down trying to work out what to do.

Trevor Ewins had a terrible accident there when he was about twelve years old. He was knocked off his bike by a car. Not surprisingly he can't remember a lot about the accident itself as he sustained head injuries. He was rushed to hospital where he had to stay for some time and then spent a further amount of time convalescing on a farm. He still has scars from this accident.

The memorial was knocked down in the end by a Triumph Herald. Luckily the driver wasn't seriously hurt but the collision left a crease right along the top of his car. After this the war memorial was rebuilt but in a less hazardous position. Some years later a re-enactment of this accident was on television.

Saltford Hall

Saltford Hall or the Village Hall or Saltford Community Association as it is known now was built by local people.

Everyone was offered the opportunity to buy a brick for six pence to help finance the building. The architect was a Mr Pope. The original hall was built on local authority land but it was later extended and the extension was on farm land. This land was known as 'Fussel's Field and was owned by Fussel's Brewery in Bristol. The brewery used to have heavy horses and they spent the summer out in the field as their holiday. Sue Brock remembered this clearly and also that cows often escaped from the fields regularly and ambled past the houses.

Both Cecil Ewins and Gordon Reed were instrumental in pushing this project on to completion.

The hall was very much fitted out with voluntary labour and Marie Carder's father helped to wire the electrics.

Saltford Hall has a mural depicting a number of real life local characters living in Saltford at the time including a dog. The person responsible for this mural was Alan Durman. Alan was an artist and created some of the well-known railway posters of the time. Residents also remember that Alan Durman used to be involved in the Saltford Carnival and one year dressed as a snake charmer and the people on the flat bed lorry with him squirted the onlookers with 'squirty' washing up liquid bottles which had just been invented at the time.

Roger Dowse remembers when only having lived in Saltford for a relatively short time being asked if he would help with the village paper collection and sorting at Saltford Hall which was a monthly event:

"I was greeted by a man who was clearly an organiser and was very definitely in charge. I soon found out that his name was Gordon Reed. Many people of a certain age will remember Gordon he was such a stalwart of village life. I was asked if I would take on a round for collection and go round with my car to pick up newspapers which people collected during the month and on the date put out by their front gate. There were quite a few rounds and Gordon had press ganged a team into place. There were always a few rounds that weren't covered and we were badgered by Gordon into doing another after finishing our own. He was not someone you could say no to, and you knew it was going to be a late night!"

The papers were sorted in the hall where a large team of volunteers put them: "into the regulation size bundles with the famous blue string. Older helpers started in the afternoon gradually being reinforced by younger volunteers after getting home from work. It was a good opportunity to meet people from the village and of course catch up on local gossip."

Roger recollects that some helpers were essential and always there: "Dick Mould with his van never stopped and his wife Ann was another stalwart. Another village stalwart was John Smee. I particularly remember Malcolm Pearce who specialised in braking up and folding the cardboard boxes. Many of the young dads who were there are still my best friends. Unfortunately it all came to an end when the bottom fell out of the market for waste paper and the SCA lost a valuable source of income."

The Women's Institute Hut

This was a wooden building on Norman Road from which many activities took place including the Evergreen's Club. Some residents remember that there was an orchard close to this building.

Saltford Men's Club

This building was located in The Shallows and had a gas fire and a snooker table. Mrs Mercer ran an old time dance class there for young people, where, amongst other dances they could learn the 'Valeta'. This building was previously a Primitive Methodist Chapel and is now a private residence.

Pubs

The Jolly Sailor

The Jolly Sailor has an interesting history as it was used as a stop off point for barge captains to spend the night. There were burnt holes all over a picture that once hung over the fire place where the barge captains had plunged the poker.

At one time, it's reputed that the landlord was a man named 'Sayward' who made off with the takings, the picture above the fireplace and the original pub sign.

"It was well frequented in the war," Trevor Ewins recalls: "as it had rooms to let. It was popular with RAF boys based at Colerne who would meet their girlfriends there."

Trevor also remembers that when he was a boy there was a tin shack extension on the side of the pub where you now go into the pub: "There was a table tennis table and a bar and this encouraged sixteen and seventeen year old boys to go in and talk to the RAF lads. A doctor from Bristol used to come over every weekend."

This extension also housed a wind-up gramophone and the Doctor would bring classical music and play it to the boys.

Trevor remembers that someone also had a Scottie dog and when it was given a saucer of beer it would scoot round and round and eventually go to sleep.

The Ship Inn

At one time the Ship Inn had been a Coaching Inn with stables on the side. The Ollis family, who originally came from Holland and were the owners of Ollis Transport, owned the Ship Inn at one time. It was situated at the bottom of Saltford Hill.

It is said that there are seventeen gravestones in the churchyard that bear the name 'Ollis'. The Ollis family were a big family and it's reputed that there were twenty two children all from the same mum.

The Bird in Hand

This pub was once run by Mrs Packer who used to sit in the upper room: "She was a right martinet with her son, Terry," one resident recalled.

Marie Carder: "On summer evenings occasionally we would go with my parents to 'The Bird in Hand' and my father would buy us lemonade and crisps from a small serving hatch at the side. We sat in the garden at the back and searched through the crisps for the salt twist of blue paper, sometimes if you were really lucky you got two twists of salt! Happy memories."

How Saltford looked from the air

Taken in 1962 there is an aerial view of the streets and buildings of Saltford as they were at that time.

This photo was taken by Malcolm Guthrie who arrived in Saltford for six months in 1957 and is still here. Malcolm had a pilot's licence and his employer needed a photo of what had been the old Douglas motorbike factory as they were taking the building over. Malcolm went up in a plane to take photos. On this trip Malcolm was accompanied by his son, Timothy.

On needing to take some shots from the passenger side Malcolm swapped places leaving his school age son in the pilot seat and under instructions to tell nobody about this little jaunt. Timothy, naturally was thrilled and proud of this experience and within the next couple of days the story was all round his school and much of Saltford.

Phases of development

Like most villages and towns Saltford has seen different phases of building development, an encroaching of open land by buildings and to some extent this has also influenced means of transport.

Marie Carder: "I remember feeding horses in Golf Club Lane before the bungalows were built and walking along the lane to Keynsham and picking mushrooms in the fields (now Montague Road and the roads leading off). We used to cycle and walk a lot then and if we wanted to go to Bath or Bristol we could take the bus, or the train from Saltford Station. Hopefully we will be able to do that again in the not too distant future."

Pat Wood recalls that Uplands Road was seen as a 'posh' road. When an estate of about fifty semi-detached houses were built people in Uplands Road were not very happy: "There was a hedge they didn't want removed because they didn't want to have to mix with the new residents. But the hedge went in the end."

Chapter Eight – More recent Years

Buzzards, road closures and proposals of marriage

Road Closure

In 2006 the A4 route through the centre of Saltford was completely closed throughout the summer.

The road was being re-surfaced due to some slight signs of subsidence but once the minor work started it was discovered that all the sewers had collapsed.

There didn't appear to be any plans showing what lay beneath the road including the main power cables: "The only way to sort the problem out was to dig up the whole road. It was a real mess," one Saltford resident remembered.

"All the mains cables had to be re-routed. Some houses had to have temporary generators."

"There was a lot of anger at first," another resident recalled. "There was a meeting at Saltford Hall and the hall was full. There were gates at each end of the road closure. People who lived in Saltford had a pass on their front windscreen and the people guarding the gates had a list of people who had been given a pass. The contractors, perhaps wisely decided to put young women on the gates because they thought they would more easily diffuse any heated situations."

One of the bus drivers was going out with one of these young women and he proposed to her at the gate while he was driving the bus: "The young woman said 'yes' and the whole bus full of people cheered!"

Village Life in the Twenty First Century

The Scouts and Guides continue to flourish in the village.

Camping, indoor holidays, abseiling, canoeing, computer skills and international trips all continue to attract new members with a wide and progressive programme.

They are always looking for new leaders to cope with their waiting lists of local children.

Saltford Community Association, which for over fifty years has looked after and enhanced the community buildings on Wedmore Road and distributed three thousand copies of the SCAN magazine every other month, has also in recent times organised every other year an ambitious nine day Festival in June. It extends to over eighty events each time, morning, afternoon and evening in and around the village and brings residents of all ages together in a very special way.

The Hall continues to be a centre of community activity for the village. As well as the mural it has also got a millennium embroidery created in the year 2000 by Barbara Butler. It still has one of the best dance floors around. It has recently installed a lift and made two thousand pounds at its Christmas Market 2014.

A 'Santa Dash' was held in Saltford for the second time in December 2014. This dash was organised by a committee connected to Saltford Sports Club and six hundred and ninety participants set off from Saltford Hall dressed up as Santa Clause. They ran a five mile course for charity, raising more than nine thousand pounds. Children also dressed as Father Christmas ran a shorter course, the youngest of which was two years of age. The oldest Santa was eighty six years of age. Three generations from the same family took part, and one lady was pushed around in her wheelchair which had been made to look like a sleigh. Seventy five teenagers took part.

Buzzards, herons, sparrow hawks, woodpeckers, jays and small birds are still seen around Saltford, though sadly no nightingales. Tawny owls are heard calling at night, and bats

fly and roost in season. Hedgehogs, badgers, slow worms and pheasants are seen occasionally in the right habitat. A pair of mallard ducks make an annual visit to Cynthia's front garden, using the bird bath before disappearing to nest somewhere unknown.

Although much flora and fauna has inevitably been lost it is nice to hear that residents now see more buzzards than they used to as Saltford strides onward into the future creating tomorrow's memories.